50

fantastic things to do with
paint

KIRSTINE BEELEY & ALISTAIR BRYCE-CLEGG

Published 2012 by Featherstone Education
Bloomsbury Publishing plc
50 Bedford Square, London, WC1B 3DP
www.bloomsbury.com

ISBN 978-1-4081-5984-2

Text © Kirstine Beeley and Alistair Bryce-Clegg 2012
Design © Lynda Murray
Photographs © Shutterstock

Printed and bound in China by C&C Offset Printing Co Ltd, Shenzhen, Guangdong
10 9 8 7 6 5 4 3 2 1

This book is produced using paper that is made from wood grown in
managed, sustainable forests. It is natural, renewable and recyclable.
The logging and manufacturing processes conform to the environmental
regulations of the country of origin.

To see our full range of titles visit www.bloomsbury.com

Acknowledgements
We would like to thank the staff and children of the following settings for their time
and patience in helping put this book together, including the use of a number of
photographs.

Treehouse Preschool, Winslow, Bucks
Prestwood Infant School, Prestwood, Bucks
MKFocus Childcare Ltd, Milton Keynes
The Arches Primary School, Blacon, Chester

Also special thanks to Fee Bryce-Clegg.

Contents

Introduction

Young children need to engage in a wide variety of experiences to help them to make sense of the world around them. The more that they can see, hear, touch and feel the better they will be at understanding all of the complex processes that are part of their everyday life. Painting with children is so much more than four primary colours in plastic pots (with matching lids)! The world around them doesn't come in only four colours so we need to make sure that we give children the opportunity to mix a variety of colours, tones and shades and the freedom to experiment with using them.

Children are naturally inquisitive and they love to experiment and explore. For them, touch is a very powerful means of finding out about how something is made and how it works. They are far more likely to use something in their play if they have been part of making or creating it. Lots of the recipes for paint in this book have been specifically chosen so that children can be involved in their creation from the start. We have also tried to include as many other sensory dimensions to the paint as we can. The more senses that are engaged in any activity, the more powerful the learning experience will be for the child.

Don't be afraid to let your children experiment with their paint mixing. It is through a series of trial and error investigations that they truly learn a skill. If they decide to make green using yellow and red paint, it is easy for us to tell them that yellow and red actually make orange and give them some green paint to use instead. It is, however, a much more powerful learning experience if we let them try out their theory and discover the result for themselves, letting them repeat the process until they get the answer they are looking for. Teaching is often about 'guiding' rather than 'telling'.

It is also really important that experimenting with colour and texture is a regular feature of the painting provision that you offer. Ultimately, you are trying to teach children a range of skills that they can practise and then go on to use when most appropriate. If they only use thick paint on special occasions it will not become a familiar choice for everyday painting, they will just connect it to that one occasion.

So, make sure that you offer your children lots of choice in the colour, thickness and texture of their paint. Let them experience making the paint and then using it through as many senses as possible. Bear in mind that your ultimate aim is for them to learn all of these techniques and to be able to apply them by choice in their artwork.

But, most of all...

...get messy and have fun!

Skin allergy alert

Some detergents and soaps can cause skin reactions.
Always be mindful of potential skin allergies when letting children mix anything with their hands and always provide facilities to wash materials off after they have been in contact with the skin. Watch out for this symbol on the relevant pages!

Food allergy alert

When using food stuffs to enhance your paint play opportunties always be mindful of potential food allergies. We have used this symbol on the relevant pages.

Balloons in a box

What you need:

- **Paper or fabric** (for creating the outside tent)
- **Tall-sided box** (such as an archive box)
- **Balloon pump** (optional)
- **Balloons**
- **Water-based paint** - if you add PVA it sticks to the balloon better

What to do:

1. Stick paper to all four sides and the bottom of the box.

2. Blow up a balloon but DON'T tie it!

3. Paint the outside of the balloon with lots of paint (this can be done in or out of the box).

4. Let go of the balloon and watch it fly around the box.

Health & Safety

Clear up all fragments of broken balloon after this activity, as they can be a choking hazard.

Taking it forward

- Try big and small boxes to see the difference.
- Try different shaped balloons.

Big it up!

- Increase the size of the balloon for a more dramatic effect.
- Create a paper or fabric tent/den outside and release multiple balloons inside it at once.

What's in it for the children?

Despite a high level of fun and engagement there are lots of links to other areas of the curriculum, particularly around investigation and discovery.

Top tip ⭐

Use a box with a handle cut into the side. Then you can hold the end of the balloon from the outside leaving the drippy painted bit of the balloon inside.

Big paint with mops

What you need:

- **Number of large trays**
- **Water-based paint**
- **Washing up liquid**
- **Paper to cover the floor** (or a tarpaulin)
- **Several mops** with both string heads and sponge heads

What to do:

1. Fill the trays with paint (add some washing up liquid for extra 'glide' and to create coloured bubbles).

2. Cover the ground with paper (or a tarpaulin if you don't want to keep your art).

3. Dampen the mops before you start (it works better with a wet mop).

4. Dip the mops into the paint and mop away!

Taking it forward

- Use the mop painting to help the children learn colours or number and letter shapes.

- Dip half of the mop in one colour and half in another and see what happens!

What's in it for the children?

Good for developing spatial awareness, balance, hand/eye coordination and upper body control. Lots of opportunities for colour mixing and observing change as the paint gets bubblier and bubblier.

Top tip ⭐

If you are mopping onto plastic or tarpaulin, you can take a relief print by pressing clean paper or fabric down onto the paint and then peeling it back.

Painting on plastic

What you need:

- A roll of decorator's plastic sheeting or a transparent umbrella
- Water soluble paint
- Washing up liquid
- Brushes or rollers in various sizes

Taking it forward

- When the children have finished painting, get as many as you can inside the structure and then either wait for rain (this could take a while) or hose down the outside and watch the colours run and mix.

What's in it for the children?

There are lots of opportunities to encourage discussion and negotiation skills in the construction of your plastic den. When the children are painting they will see how the paint behaves differently when it is applied to plastic as opposed to paper. They also get the chance to 'mirror paint' and copy whoever is standing on the other side of the plastic. As light shines through the painting on the inside and outside the children will see the colours mix.

Top tip ⭐

Add a bit of washing up liquid to your paint to help it wash off more easily.

What to do:

1. Wrap the plastic around any large structure that you have in your outdoor area (like a climbing frame).

2. If there's not an obvious 'structure' get the children to build one using crates and blocks.

3. Make sure that you leave a hole for the children to get in and out of their newly constructed plastic house/den!

4. With various sized brushes and rollers you can paint from both the inside and the outside at the same time.

Handy hint
You can buy plastic sheeting from most DIY shops. Choose one on a roll that's thinner and easier to work with.

Big rollers and brushes

What you need:

- Paint trays
- Paint of different consistencies
- Large pieces of paper such as lining paper
- Large decorating rollers
- Roller extension handles
- Emulsion brushes

What to do:

1. Get the children to fill the paint trays with paint of various thicknesses.
2. Attach large pieces of paper to a wall, fence or the ground.
3. Use the rollers and brushes to make big movements.

Taking it forward

- Use different textures of roller to get a different paint effect.
- Add an extension handle to the roller for a different challenge.
- Tape your brushes to the end of sticks for extra reach.

What's in it for the children?

Not only do the children get to explore all the elements of colour and texture they are also developing their upper body muscles, balance and hand/eye coordination and producing a work of art as a bonus!

Tuff tray spinners

What you need:

- String
- Builders' tray or tuff spot
- Strong tape
- Washing line
- Water based paint

What to do:

1. Take four pieces of string of equal length (approx. 150cm).

2. Attach one piece to each corner of the tuff spot tray.

3. Take the loose ends and knot them together, try to keep the strings of equal length.

Handy hint
You could drill some holes in the corners of your tuff tray and tie your string on rather than tape it on.

4. Peg, tape or tie the knotted strings to your washing line (your tray should now be hanging in mid-air).

5. Cover the bottom of the tray with paper.

6. Get the children to squeeze blobs of paint into the middle of the tray.

7. Spin the tray!

Taking it forward

- Try using paint of different consistencies.
- Try adding paint while the tray is spinning.

What's in it for the children?

This activity always has a high level of engagement. It explores lots of elements of science particularly forces.

Top tip ⭐

Keep your strings nice and long so that the children can see the paint spin.

Blow paint

What you need:

- **An eye dropper** is useful but not essential
- **Non-toxic paint heavily watered down**
- **Straws**
- **Plain paper**

What to do:

1. Use the dropper to put the paint onto the paper.
2. Instead of a dropper you could drip paint off the end of a straw.
3. Select a straw.
4. Blow!

Handy hint

Piercing the straws with a pin near the top should help prevent children from drinking paint!

Top tip ★

Practise first to avoid paint consumption!

Taking it forward

- Have collaborative blow painting where a number of children are blowing the same blob (or different blobs) at the same time!
- Have paint blowing races.
- Cover light items, such as ping pong balls, in paint and blow them over paper to create a pattern.
- Turn your blow paint shapes into creatures by adding googly eyes and other features.

Big it up!

- Use a hair dryer (set to cool) for larger scale work.
- Blow up a balloon (hold it tightly) and use the expelling air to blow your paint.

What's in it for the children?

Children will be exploring cause and effect, as well as some early physics, as they make their breath move the paint. Try letting them blow without a straw and see what a difference this makes. Alongside being scientists they are also learning how to paint with air.

Cars and trucks

What to do:

1. Roll the cars and trucks through a tray of paint.
2. 'Drive' them across the paper to create a pattern.

Handy hint

Make sure you have a 'car wash' nearby for those who want clean wheels before they roll!

Taking it forward

- Introduce other concepts such as colour recognition and repeated pattern. Can the children give the red cars red wheels and the blue ones blue wheels? You could ask them to make a simple repeated pattern of red and blue tracks or something more complex using more colours.

- Have a variety of different sized vehicles available.

- Try and choose cars and trucks with different patterns on their tyres so that children can match or guess which vehicle made which pattern.

Big it up!

- Take it outside and use the wheeled toys. Paint their wheels and ride them over large sheets of paper.

- Let the children paint old car or bike tyres and then roll on paper outside to show the different tracks. (See also **Tyre and wheel painting** page 57).

What's in it for the children?

This is a great opportunity to explore colour and colour mixing. This activity also provides the opportunity to introduce skills such as pattern matching and discussing size and shape.

Top tip ⭐

Painting small wheels with a brush is difficult so make sure your paint tray is long enough for the car's wheels to make a full turn before they are used for painting.

Painting with a wet fish!

What you need:

- Whole fish (dead!)
- Water-based paint
- Fingers, brushes or rollers
- Sugar paper

What to do:

1. Give the children time to examine and investigate the fish. (Be mindful of cultural and religious preferences when using food stuffs.)

2. Paint the entire fish with the water based paint.

3. Cover with sugar paper.

4. Press the paper all over.

5. Peel back the paper to reveal a detailed relief print of the fish.

FOOD allergy!

Handy hint
Sugar paper works best because it's so porous. Try using contrasting paint and paper colours like black and white.

Taking it forward

- Get the children to experiment with different types of paper and paint and see what effects they can produce.

- Paint the fish with a light coating of oil and try tissue paper or brown paper.

Big it up!

- Create a shoal using different types of papers and paint.

What's in it for the children?

The children get a unique opportunity to explore the natural world whilst also finding out about the properties of relief printing. Don't forget that you are introducing the children to a new process so don't restrict their experience to fish. Get them to try relief printing with a number of different things.

Top tip ⭐

Use a large flat fish for the best effect.

Making glitter paint

What you need:

- Wallpaper paste
- Water
- Food colouring/powder paint
- Glitter

What to do:

1. Mix the water and the wallpaper paste according to the instructions.

2. Add the food colouring if you want a clear paint.

3. Add the powder paint if you want an opaque paint.

4. Add glitter of your choice.

Health & Safety

Make sure you buy the paste **WITHOUT** the anti-fungal ingredient. Check packaging for details.

Taking it forward

- Add different sparkly things to your paint like sequins and chopped up tinsel.

- Add glitter to PVA glue. When the glue dries it will dry clear just leaving a glittery trail.

- Mix glitter, PVA glue and powder paint to get a 'gloss' finish to your paint when it dries.

Big it up!

This mixture can also be used as an experiential activity if you make it in larger quantities, put it into a tray or bowl and add larger shinier things like tinsel and Lametta. Great for getting your hands really glittery and gooey!

What's in it for the children?

Good for developing spatial awareness, balance, hand/eye coordination and upper body control. Lots of opportunities for colour mixing and observing change as the paint gets bubblier and bubblier.

Top tip ⭐

Adding powder paint will make the paint even thicker so make sure you add more water.

Painting with a stick brush

What you need:

- Mud paint (see page 20) or water based paint
- Variety of sticks
- Long grass cuttings, straw or hay
- Tape or twine to bind
- Paper

What to do:

1. Select a stick.
2. Sort out a good handful of long pieces of grass, hay or straw. Fold them in half.
3. Attach the folded end of the grass to one end of the stick using tape or twine.
4. Repeat instructions 2 to 4 until the end of the stick is covered.
5. Dip your brush into the mud or water paint and drag it across a variety of papers and different surfaces.

Handy hint

The longer the grass, hay or straw the better – you can always trim it once it's finished.

Taking it forward

- Try long and short sticks.
- Use a variety of grasses (fresh and dried) and compare the results.
- Ask the children to find alternatives to grass such as leaves and twigs.

Big it up!

- For some brilliant gross motor upper body work, make your brushes the size of broomsticks and then get to work on some gigantic pieces of paper!

What's in it for the children?

Children will have to use their higher order thinking skills to make this activity work. They will also be developing both their fine and gross motor skills in putting the brush together and then using it.

Top tip ⭐

Attaching the grass to the end of the stick can be a bit fiddly for little fingers so get children working in pairs or with an adult.

Paint on warm stones with wax

What you need:

- Large stones
- Wax crayons
- Number of large trays
- An oven

What to do:

1. Warm the stones in the oven.

2. Let the children draw on the warm stones with wax crayons.

Taking it forward

- Try using other things such as pastels and chalk – do they all have the same effect?

Big it up!

- For a larger scale piece of art, turn a baking tray upside down and put a hot water bottle underneath it. The water bottle should be hot but not boiling. The heat of the bottle will warm the tray.

- Put a piece of paper onto the warm surface and then allow the children to draw on it with wax crayons. The hot water bottle should have made the baking tray warm enough to melt the wax and also should help to retain the heat.

What's in it for the children?

This is a lovely activity for exploring texture, the smoothness of the melting wax over the roughness of the stones. It is a good opportunity for language development and it allows children to use natural materials in a unique way.

Top tip ★

If the stones cool down too much you can just return them to the oven, warm them up a bit and carry on.

Icing sugar paint

What you need:

- **Icing sugar**
- **Water**
- **Ready-mixed paint**
- **Coloured ink**
- **Food colouring**
- **Glitter**
- This effect works best on **smooth white paper**, but will produce an effect on most surfaces

What to do:

1. Mix icing sugar and water in a paint pot until you get a runny consistency.

2. Paint this sugar and water solution all over the surface. (Use plenty of solution so that the surface is fairly wet and won't dry too quickly).

3. Drop ready-mixed paint, ink or food colouring on to the wet surface.

4. Sprinkle with glitter.

5. Watch as the colour explodes like a firework as it hits the paper.

Handy hint

Allow plenty of drying time. This solution takes longer to dry than conventional paint.

Taking it forward

- Experiment with different quantities of paint, ink or food colouring.

- Drop different colours next to each other and watch how they merge and mix to create new colours.

Big it up!

On a large piece of paper, apply the solution with a paint roller and encourage groups of children to flick paint to create a piece of collaborative art.

What's in it for the children?

This paint effect has just a little bit of magic as the drops of paint spread like an exploding firework. If you are using lots of different paint colours there are opportunities to discuss colour mixing and also make links with other experiences that children may have had such as fireworks or fairy lights.

Painting with oil

What you need:

- **Vegetable oil**
- **Powder paint** (optional)
- **Container with an air tight lid**
- **Variety of papers** (thin papers such as tissue paper or brown paper work best)

What to do:

1. Put a little oil into a container and brush onto your selected paper.

2. Now add powder paint to the oil and shake vigorously. Brush onto your selected paper.

Handy hint

Pure oil will not leave a colour on the paper but make the areas painted appear more translucent.

Taking it forward

- Experiment with a number of types of paper.
- Try using tin foil – what happens to that?
- Paint with oil onto fabric and see how its appearance changes.

Big it up!

As oil on paper tends to make it appear more translucent, this is a great effect to use when you are creating large scale artwork that is going to hang on or in front of a window.

What's in it for the children?

This is a gloriously slippery medium for children to work in. It feels great, not only when being applied to paper, but also against their skin. There is lots of science involved in using oil to paint with especially if you get the children to try it on a non-porous surface like tin foil.

Top tip ⭐

Oil and water don't mix so if you want to colour your oil you have to use powder paint. To stop the powder from forming lumps in the oil, be prepared to really shake it!

Mud paint

What you need:

- Soil
- Paint pots or beakers
- Water
- Food colouring
- Card for painting on

What to do:

1. Put your soil into paint pots or beakers to make mixing easier.

2. If you want smooth paint pick out any stones or lumps.

3. Slowly add water and stir until creamy (you can now just use like this).

4. Add some drops of food colouring to your mud (you will see the difference in colour when you paint with it).

Handy hint

If you are painting with textured mud, paint onto card as paper is not strong enough to support the lumps!

Taking it forward

- Use your 'smooth' mud as you would normal paint.
- Try 'dolloping' your textured mud onto cardboard to create mud piles.
- Pour your mud paint over other objects such as bits of egg box to produce a 3D mud picture.

Big it up!

- This paint is great for long distance splatting which helps to develop children's balance, hand eye coordination and upper body. You can paint the tyres of your wheeled toys with it and get the children to ride them across large sheets of paper to create a huge piece of pattern art.
- For large-scale mud paintings, attach bunches of grass, straw or hay to the end of a stick and use as a paintbrush (see page 16).

What's in it for the children?

Alongside all of the language and texture development, this is a lovely activity for encouraging children to be creative with what they have around them – using natural materials to create art.

Top tip ⭐

The more clay based your soil the lighter shade of mud paint you will get.

Paint on bark

What you need:

- Paint or natural ink
- Pieces of bark (the bigger the better)
- Brushes, sponges, fingers...

What to do:

1. The outside of the bark is usually rough with lots of crevices and holes. Children can experiment with using different painting techniques and utensils to see if they can cover the space.

2. The inside of bark is often lighter in colour and smoother. It gives an opportunity for an almost opposite experience and the use of other painting utensils.

Taking it forward

- Find other rough and smooth surfaces in both the indoor and outdoor environment.

Big it up!

- Use a large bit of bark from the trunk of a felled or fallen tree for a piece of collaborative art.
- Join lots of individual pieces of 'bark art' to form a large natural sculpture or piece of artwork.

What's in it for the children?

This activity gives children an opportunity to explore natural materials at close range and also to experiment with the use of a variety of painting implements and paint techniques.

Top tip ★

Your local tree surgeon should be able to provide you with large and small pieces of bark.

Grass, nut or berry paints

What you need:

- One of the following:
  - grass
  - leaves
  - moss
  - raspberries
  - blueberries
  - beetroot
  - red cabbage
  - nut shells (such as walnut)
  – the list is endless…
- Pan
- Water
- Sieve

What to do:

1. Put whatever you are going to use to make your paint in the pan. You can literally use anything. Half of the fun is experimenting! The more paint you want, the more you need to use.

2. If your ingredients are hard (like nut shells or berries) add just enough water to cover them.

3. If your ingredients are leafy like moss or grass then add two cups of water to start with and then keep your eye on it!

4. Bring to the boil and then simmer for 45 minutes (DON'T boil dry).

5. When cooled strain through a sieve.

Handy hint

Try the colour first as it may be different from the colour of the thing you used. Beetroot makes yellow ink!

Health & Safety

Remind children not to pick berries or lick their fingers during this activity.

Top tip ⭐

For some ingredients you only need to add a little to get a very vivid colour (like walnut shells). For others you need a large quantity for a paler colour (like grass).

Taking it forward

- You can make the painting ink colour tie in with the seasons.

- Get children to scavenge outdoors for their own ingredients.

- Let children mix a variety of ingredients to see what they get.

What's in it for the children?

Making this painting ink is a lovely way of getting the children to engage with their outdoor environment. Talking about what might happen is good for developing children's thinking and predicting skills especially as some of the results might challenge their thinking – and yours!

Big it up!

Make links to literature through your creative work. Inspire the children with books like '*In the Witches' Kitchen*' and make a huge cauldron of painting ink for the children to use to write spells and paint pictures.

Paint on bread

What you need:

- Food colouring
- Milk
- Brushes
- Bread (white)

What to do:

1. Mix various food colourings with a little milk.
2. Paint the food colouring and milk mixture onto a slice of bread.
3. Toast the bread.
4. Eat your toasty masterpiece!

FOOD allergy !

Health & Safety

Always make sure using the toaster is an 'adult only' activity.

Taking it forward

- You can link this activity to other aspects of your teaching. You could re-enforce colour recognition by colour coding your toast.

- Get the children to practise letter formation by putting their initials on the bread.

Big it up!

- Use lots of slices of toast art to create an original (and edible) display. If you want your toast to last for a long time, paint it with varnish.

What's in it for the children?

Children and adults always enjoy this one – there is nothing more satisfying than painting your own snack! Not only does it create high level engagement, you can also link it to many other areas of the curriculum like mathematics. Not only can you cut your bread into simple shapes like circles and triangles you can also number the slices. That way you need to order your snack before you eat it!

Top tip ⭐

Don't make your bread too wet with the milky paint otherwise it won't toast and so doesn't taste too great!

Pumpkin painting

What you need:

- **Water based paint** in a variety of colours and finishes
- **Small pots**
- **Spoons**
- **PVA glue**
- **Pumpkins** (or any large fruit or vegetables)

What to do:

1. Sort your paint into pots.
2. Add a spoonful of PVA glue to each pot.
3. Put your pumpkin on newspaper or a paper plate.
4. Spoon different paints onto the top of the pumpkin and let them slowly drip down the sides.

Taking it forward

- Use fruit and vegetables that are seasonal, making a link to Understanding the World.

- Link colours of seasons and festivals to the fruit you are painting. Summer fruit might get hot colours, whereas winter vegetables might get cold colours. Halloween pumpkins might be painted in purple, orange and black.

Big it up!

Stack up your fruit and vegetables to create a larger display where children can work collectively. If the fruit and vegetables are stacked one on top of the other then you get a whole new effect as a number of different paints combine on the way down.

What's in it for the children?

Children are getting the opportunity to use everyday objects in a different way. Children might be encountering some fruit and vegetables for the first time. This activity gives them a chance for a sensory experience rather than being asked to taste them straight away.

Top tip ★

Use metallic paint for a different kind of effect.

Paint with a roller ball

What you need:

- Old roller ball deodorant bottles
- Water based paint
- Washing up liquid
- Paper in a variety of textures

Taking it forward

- These are best used on a horizontal surface.
- This activity is great for consolidating and developing the use of the upper body in mark making.

Big it up!

Employ the same principle on a larger scale by using child-sized line markers. These can be purchased from educational suppliers (such as TTS).

What's in it for the children?

This activity helps children to explore large scale movement and consolidate and develop their upper body dexterity.

Top tip ⭐

Use a squirt of washing up liquid to help the ball to run smoothly.

What to do:

1. Cut a hole in the bottom of your deodorant bottle, about the size of a felt tip pen.
2. Wash and rinse it out.
3. Fill with paint.
4. Add a squirt of washing up liquid.
5. Fill hole with a felt tip pen lid.
6. Paint!

Handy hint

Use the felt tip lid to fill the hole that matches the colour of paint in the bottle.

Paint with rubber gloves

What you need:

- Rubber gloves
- Water based paint
- Funnel
- Darning needle
- Pegs

Taking it forward

- Change the number and size of the holes.
- Use the funnel to put a different colour in each finger.
- Instead of pegging your glove, blow into it and see what happens.

Big it up!

- Use different sized plastic bags instead of gloves.

What's in it for the children?

This activity uses lots of fine motor skills to get the paint inside the gloves and then some fine and gross motor ones to get it back out again. Children will learn about how it is the force of them squeezing on the glove that makes the paint shoot out through the holes.

Top tip ★

To make filling your gloves easier, cut a 2l drinks bottle in half. Put the 'fingers' end of your glove inside the bottom half of the bottle and then stretch the 'wrist' end around the outside (like putting your socks over the top of your wellies)!

What to do:

1. Make a hole (or two) in each finger of the rubber glove.

2. Use the funnel to pour paint into the glove – a little may leak out of the fingers **(DO NOT SQUEEZE!)**

3. Twist the glove at the wrist and put a peg around the twist to keep it shut.

4. Squeeze!

Health & Safety

Be aware that some children might be allergic to latex so have latex-free gloves available.

Handy hint

Paint will shoot out at all angles, especially if you have got lots of holes in your glove, so be prepared!

Super thick slime paint

What you need:

- **Cellulose powder** (find this in an educational supplier catalogue or on the internet)
- **Water**
- **Food colouring or powder paint**

What to do:

1. Mix the water and the cellulose power according to the instructions. If you want it SUPER thick then add less water.
2. Leave it for a few hours to thicken (best overnight).
3. Add your food colouring if you want translucent slime paint.
4. Add powder paint if you want a more vivid colour.

Handy hint

Adding powder paint will make the paint even thicker so make sure you add more water.

Taking it forward

- Mix a variety of textured paint for use in the same picture.
- Leave your paint overnight to see how it changes.
- Use a variety of different textured papers (e.g. wallpaper, sandpaper, tin foil) for the children to paint on to. How does the paint act differently?

Big it up!

This paint is great for throwing and splatting against large pieces of paper. Its slimy texture makes it ideal for painting using hands and feet. Try funneling it into a deflated balloon, blowing it up then popping it onto paper. Add items to it like glitter, sequins, plastic flies or toy creepy crawlies…

What's in it for the children?

Making this paint feels like a real scientific experiment. It offers lots of opportunities to experience its unique texture and also to develop descriptive language. Due to its sliminess this is often a popular one with the boys!

Top tip ★

If you can't get cellulose powder you can get a similar (if a little stickier) effect with wallpaper paste. Make sure you buy the paste WITHOUT the anti-fungal ingredient.

Painting with tea bags

What you need:

- **Tea bags**
- **Water based paint**
- **Paper**
- **Space** on the floor or wall to make a mess!

What to do:

1. Rinse your teabags out in boiling water two or three times (you don't want the colour of the tea).

2. Dip a wet teabag into a paint colour of your choice.

3. Throw it up in the air and watch it splat on the floor.

4. Throw it away from your body and watch it splat against a wall.

Handy hint

Use plastic tongs to grab and dip your teabags. This is good for reinforcing pincer grip and hand/eye coordination.

Taking it forward

- Use a spoon or ruler to 'launch' your teabags even further and with more force.

- Try dipping different sides of your teabag in different coloured paint for a colour mixing effect.

- Paint your paper with a solution of icing sugar and water before launching your teabag for an even more dramatic paint effect.

Big it up!

Create huge teabag art outside on large sheets of paper. Launch your teabags from different heights and see if this makes a difference to the paint effect.

What's in it for the children?

The children will have an opportunity to explore materials and their properties, from the changes in the teabag when it goes from dry to wet to how it changes again when soaked in paint. Examining how throwing a teabag at different speeds and from different heights affects the pattern that it makes, helps children to begin to explore cause and effect (as well as a bit of gravity)!

Top tip ★

Pyramid-shaped teabags are the easiest to work with.

Textured paint

What you need:

- **Powder paint or ready mixed paint** (or make your own)
- **Large container for mixing**
- **Textures to add to your paint.** Try: sand, sawdust, porridge, rice, lentils... anything with a bit of texture!
- **Large brushes, spatulas, lolly sticks to apply your paint with**
- **Paper**

Taking it forward

- Mix a variety of textured paint for use in the same picture.

- Leave your paint overnight to see how it changes.

- Use a variety of different textured papers (e.g. wallpaper, sandpaper, tin foil) for the children to paint onto. How does the paint act differently?

Top tip ⭐

Added ingredients like porridge and rice will absorb lots of the moisture from the paint so you may need to get the children to add more water as they go.

What to do:

1. Allow the children to select the colour of paint that they would like to use.

2. Keep the paint fairly thick. You can always water it down after you have added the texture.

3. Add your chosen texture a little at a time.

FOOD allergy !

4. Use fingers, hands and other utensils to apply the paint to the paper.

5. Leave lots of drying time! The thicker the texture the longer it will take to dry.

6. Add some flavouring or scented oil to your textured paint to make it 'scratch and sniff'.

Big it up!

Why not add PVA glue to thick textured paint and use it to create models or a 3D effect on your paintings? (This works better on a flat surface as opposed to an easel – unless you want to paint the floor!)

What's in it for the children?

An activity like this not only expands children's knowledge of materials and their properties but also encourages them to investigate change and cause and effect. They have to use their ingenuity to apply the paint to the surface that they are painting and will be able to experience a range of textures and smells.

Fizzy paint

What you need:

- **Ready mixed or powder paint**
- **Small containers** (such as a shot glass or an old film case)
- **Pack of fizzing indigestion tablets**
- **Water**

What to do:

1. Arrange your containers on a large piece of paper.
2. Mix paint and water to fill ¾ of the container.
3. Drop an indigestion tablet into each container and wait for the bubbles.

Handy hint

This can sometimes be a little slow to get going and might need a little shake!

Taking it forward

- You can add glitter to your mix for a bit of sparkle!
- For a more immediate (and smelly) fizz, mix vinegar with your paint and add a teaspoon of bicarbonate of soda.

Big it up!

For a really big and very visible version use a jam jar. Just make sure to increase the number of indigestion tablets!

What's in it for the children?

Because this activity works in stages the children get the opportunity to see how a process works. The paint effect happens because of a chemical reaction between the water and the indigestion tablet so the children are experiencing early chemistry first hand. There are lots of opportunities for language development with all of the fizzing and bubbling.

Top tip ⭐

If your diluted paint produces an effect that is a bit washed out and pale add some food colouring to your mix and this will give a much brighter result.

Paint with tights

What you need:

- Tights or pop socks
- Cotton wool
- Water based paint
- Paper to cover wall/floor inside or out!

What to do:

1. Cut the legs off your tights.
2. Soak a large ball of cotton wool in a paint of your choice.
3. Put the paint-soaked ball into the foot of the tights.
4. Swing over you head and splat against the wall or floor.
5. Don't forget to wear an apron (shower cap optional although sometimes useful!)

Handy hint

Loop the end of the tights around the child's wrist to avoid UFTs (unidentified flying tights)!

Taking it forward

- Use more than one coloured tight at the same time.
- Have longer and shorter ones and see the different size of splat.
- 'Splat and drag' to get a different sort of paint effect.

Big it up!

- Try making huge splatter circles outside by swinging your tight around your head and your body. Can you make a circle?
- Try a sponge ball in a string bag. What happens?

What's in it for the children?

There's so much for the children to discover here: How the tight stretches more when the paint makes the cotton wool heavier. How the paint makes it out of the tight. The different shapes the splats make when you use a long or a short tight. How far the paint can travel while the tight is flying through the air. What is it that's squeezing the paint out?

Top tip ⭐

There is potential for paint to go far and wide (including the ceiling) so best done outside.

String and spaghetti

What you need:

- Poster paint
- A selection of wide dishes or trays
- String — different lengths and thicknesses, different types (parcel string, garden twine, jute cord, rope, raffia etc)
- Cooked, drained spaghetti
- Paper — a variety of colours, shapes and sizes

Taking it forward

- Try adding PVA glue to the paint and then leave the string on the paper to dry.
- Explore the patterns you can make with other objects dipped in paint (try cotton reels, dry spaghetti or tinsel).

Big it up!

- Have a go at dipping large skipping ropes into paint trays and dragging them across super sized pieces of paper.
- Or explore flinging painted spaghetti at large pieces of paper (just like Spiderman and his web slinging!).

What's in it for the children?

Painting with bendy materials helps children to build their hand eye co-ordination as they control the swirls of the spaghetti and string. Incorporate early science concepts by using vocabulary such as bendy, stretchy, winding, curly etc as the children paint.

What to do:

1. Place a variety of different coloured paints into the dishes or trays.

2. Choose a length of string or spaghetti (make sure you point out that the spaghetti is for painting with NOT eating!) and drag it slowly through the paint dish so it becomes covered in paint.

FOOD allergy!

3. Now draw the string across the paper leaving a long paint trail.

4. Try again with different colours, other lengths and other thicknesses.

Health & Safety
Always dispose of spaghetti carefully after use as in warm settings food bacteria can grow.

5. Encourage children to talk about the shapes and patterns they are making as well as what they see happening as the colours overlap and begin to mix.

Blat! Splat!

What you need:

- **Large sheets of paper and/or a large white sheet**
- **Masking tape**
- **A selection of different coloured water-based paints**
- **Water**
- **Funnels and jugs**
- **Balloons** – cheap party ones work best
- **Kitchen towel**

Taking it forward

- Scrunch up sheets of kitchen towel and soak them in watery paint – throw as hard as you can at the paper. This is a good one to use on a vertical canvas against a wall and makes a great throwing/target practice activity!

- Try filling the balloons with slightly less paint. Tie off and then roll the small balloon balls in paint and bounce them on your paper – they are less likely to pop and more likely to bounce around!

What's in it for the children?

A great way to build gross motor skills in shoulders, elbows and wrists (all useful in early writing) as well as getting creative on a massive scale. Children need opportunities to revisit skills in a wide variety of situations and on a variety of scales.

What to do:

1. Stick plenty of sheets of paper together using masking tape to make a massive single canvas and lay it out on a flat surface outdoors. Alternatively, spread out a large white sheet and secure the edges using logs or pebbles.

2. Carefully fill the balloons with watery paint mixtures using the funnel and a jug (they need to be quite full to ensure the latex explodes upon impact!).

3. Tie the balloons up. Repeat for more balloons using a selection of different coloured paints.

4. Throw the balloons at the paper... hard!

5. They should explode upon impact and create an impressive splat painting. If they don't explode first time try and try again!

Health & Safety

Clear up all fragments of broken balloon after this activity, as they can be a choking hazard.

Top tip ★

This is one to cover up from head to toe! Try covering the children with cheap clear emergency rain macs. They provide full covering, have a hood and can be cut to size with scissors!

Paint with chocolate!

What you need:

- **A selection of cheap chocolate bars** – plain, milk and white
- **Vegetable oil**
- **Microwaveable bowl**
- **Spoon**
- **Brushes and sponges** of different shapes and sizes
- **Small containers** such as cottage cheese tubs
- **Greaseproof paper**

What to do:

1. Break each chocolate bar into small pieces, place in a microwave proof container and melt in the microwave (30 sec blasts followed by a quick stir works best and avoids burning the chocolate). Alternatively, melt the chocolate slowly in a glass bowl over a pan of warm water. This is an adult activity.

   FOOD allergy !

2. Add a couple of teaspoons of vegetable oil to the chocolate and put it well away from the children to allow it to cool down. Repeat for various types of chocolate.

   Health & Safety
   Keep children away from the hot chocolate and warm saucepans at all times.

3. Pour the chocolate sauce into smaller containers (cottage cheese tubs are ideal).

4. Allow children to paint onto the greaseproof paper with the chocolate using brushes and sponges.

Taking it forward

- Try drizzling larger amounts of one type of chocolate onto the paper and then a blob of a different type. Allow children to drag straws through the chocolate to make and mix patterns.

- Paint with other foodstuffs including chocolate spread, jam and lemon curd.

Big it up!

Why not make up bigger mixing bowls of chocolate syrup (use ice cream sauce if it's easier) and let children get their hands in and hand paint onto larger pieces of greaseproof paper or Perspex.

What's in it for the children?

Early science asks that children explore the world using all of their senses. What better way to explore than using taste, smell and touch? This is an exciting activity that is sure to spark conversation and develop children's language. This activity also gives children the confidence to experiment with creative tools such as paintbrushes, sponges and rollers with materials other than traditional paint.

Top tip ⭐

Adding vegetable oil helps the chocolate to stay smooth and stops it from hardening quickly.

Edible art

What you need:

- **Food colourings** in a variety of colours
- **Paintbrushes** – new (or sterilized in boiling water)
- **Small bowls**
- **Water**
- **A4 rice paper sheets** (available cheaply from cooking shops or online auction websites)

What to do:

1. Mix up some food colouring with water to make your edible paints (alternatively use condensed milk or milk). Mix colours together to give you a wider paint palette.

2. Paint straight onto the rice paper – being careful not to make it too wet, as the paper will dissolve or tear.

3. Dry the paintings. (You now have a potentially fully edible painting!)

FOOD allergy !

Health & Safety
Always adhere to good food hygiene practices and be mindful of potential food allergies

Taking it forward

- Try painting on bread (see page 24).
- Paint onto rolled white icing and leave to harden.
- Make biscuits in a variety of shapes and once they have been baked and cooled paint with food colouring paints.

What's in it for the children?

This is a lovely way of exploring some unusual materials whilst making the most of developing mark making opportunities. A real multi-sensory exploration with a fun, fully edible end product.

Top tip ★

Place a piece of absorbent kitchen towel underneath your rice paper to absorb any excess paint.

Tickly time

What you need:

- **A wide selection of feathers** (available from craft shops and online). Make sure you have different colours, lengths, thickness and textures – some are smooth whilst others are really fluffy.

- **Shallow bowls or trays**

- **Water-based paint in a variety of colours**

What to do:

1. Provide the children with lots of different feathers to choose from.

SKIN allergy!

2. Fill the bowls/trays with different coloured paints and let the children dip the feathers in.

3. Paint away!

4. Encourage the children to use either end of the feathers to paint. Some are better used almost like quills with their tips dipped in and others, like peacock feathers, lend themselves to long sweeping brush-like movements.

Taking it forward

- Use watery paint mixtures to see paints blending together.

- Try spreading thick paint onto paper or another smooth surface and use the quill end of the feather (the hard end) to make marks in the paint. Press another piece of paper over the top to take a relief print.

What's in it for the children?

Children should be given lots of opportunities to mark make using instruments other then pens and pencils and this is an ideal example. It also provides a very tactile, as well as visual stimulus. The sweeping movements of the feathers encourage children to build up their hand-eye coordination skills whilst mastering bendy tools.

Top tip ⭐

If using feathers you have found or collected yourself, make sure they have been fully washed and dried before use.

Foamy fun

What you need:

- **Shaving foam and/or bath play foam** (tends to be a bit thicker and can come in other colours)
- **Clean, smooth surface** (a large tray or table top)
- **Paint in a variety of colours**
- **Variety of textures tools** including brushes, sticks, combs, shower sponges
- **Paper**
- **Glitter (optional)**

What to do:

1. Squirt some foam onto the tray or table and let the children explore with their hands and fingers.

2. Now pour some paint into the foam and let them swirl it around and mix it in. If working on a tabletop or in a builder's tray, squirt different colours on different parts of the tray/table.

3. Let children explore the foam with the texture tools to make patterns (a relief print can be taken by gently placing a piece of paper over the pattern).

Taking it forward

- Add more than one colour at a time and allow children to mix it up.
- Add coloured glitter for a sparkly foam paint.

Big it up!

Have a go at mixing up foam paints in a big builder's tray or even a paddling pool (don't let children climb in as it will be VERY slippery). Use large objects such as toilet brushes (unused!) and washing up mops to make marks in the foam.

What's in it for the children?

This is a really multi-sensory exploration of paint and a great way of building early mark making skills as children can scrape marks, letters and numerals as well as beautiful patterns. Great for developing motor skills on a larger scale.

Top tip ⭐

For children who don't like putting their hands in the foam, put paint and some foam into a zip up food bag and allow them to explore making patterns.

ALL soaked up

What you need:

- Droppers, pipettes and straws
- Watery paints made with food colouring and water
- Sheets of white kitchen towel
- Newspaper or absorbent material to cover work surface

What to do:

1. Fill your dropper or pipette with watery paint.
2. Hold over a piece of kitchen towel.
3. Let a drop or two fall onto the towel – watch the colours spread as the towel absorbs the paint.
4. Add more paint in different colours and see what happens.
5. When finished, place the sheets somewhere to dry out.

Taking it forward

- Try repeating the same activity using coffee filter papers.
- Draw circles of felt pen into the kitchen towel then drop clear water on to see what patterns you make.

What's in it for the children?

This is a nice opportunity to explore using droppers and pipettes as tools for creativity and for exploring new surfaces for creating on. This is a great activity for encouraging the language of colours and colour mixing as well as the early science of wet and dry materials.

Top tip ⭐

Be careful when transporting wet paper paintings as soggy paper can tear easily! Putting a piece of plain white copy paper under your kitchen towel will allow you to pick up the copy paper without tearing the tissue on top and allow it to be moved somewhere for drying.

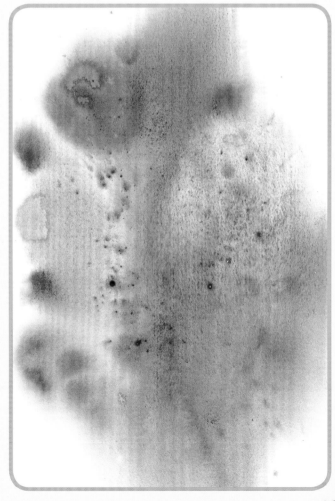

All iced up

What you need:

- **Water-based paint in a variety of colours**
- **Water**
- **Ice cube trays**
- **Lolly sticks** (craft ones will do as children will not be eating this activity!)
- **Clean yoghurt pots**
- **Access to a freezer**

What to do:

1. Mix up the paint and water (about 50/50 mix should ensure a bright enough paint which still freezes and melts reasonably quickly).

2. Pour some of your mixture into the ice cube trays (make a selection of different colours).

3. Poke a lolly stick through the bottom of a yoghurt pot and seal the edges with modeling clay or sticky tack. Pour in some coloured paint mixture and stand the pots on a foil tray or freezable plate.

4. Freeze your paint lollies and cubes.

5. When frozen, remove and use on paper to push around and make patterns. Watch the patterns change as the ice melts.

Taking it forward

- Freeze a small amount of paint then add another colour, freeze and repeat to produce rainbow ice paints which change colour as they melt.

- Add sequins or glitter to the paint for added sparkly effect.

- Try adding salt to a cluster of ice paint cubes (they will temporarily melt and then refreeze together creating a mixed ice paint cluster!).

Big it up!

Freeze cubes of paint ice on a bigger scale using take-away containers, plastic cups and bowls. Allow children to use them outside on huge pieces of paper or in a builder's tray lined with paper.

What's in it for the children?

This activity has lots of early science exploration of materials and their melting/freezing properties. It develops lots of science-based language around cold, melting etc.

Top tip ⭐

Place an absorbent cloth under your paper, as it can get very soggy as the ice melts.

Painting on shiny surfaces

What you need:

- Food colouring in a variety of colours
- Water
- Brushes
- Tin foil squares, Perspex sheets or mirrors
- Vegetable oil
- Droppers, pipettes and straws
- Kitchen roll
- Paper

What to do:

1. Make up some 'paints' using food colouring and water.
2. Paint directly onto foil squares – watch as the paint clumps together in blobs.
3. Mix in some vegetable oil and see if you can spread the paint out more. As oil and water don't mix, the children will see them separating as well as the food colour tinting the oil.
4. Use droppers to add more 'paint' of different colours – do they mix?
5. Can you blow the paints around using the straws?
6. Place a piece of kitchen towel or paper over the foil and see if you can lift off a print.

Taking it forward

- Add more water to the shiny surface before swirling your paint around.
- Add flour, cornflour or sand and see what happens now.
- Add PVA glue and see if it covers better.

What's in it for the children?

Children need lots of opportunities to explore the properties of different materials as they play. This is a fun way of exploring the properties of water and oil and seeing what happens when they mix together, as well as exploring the use of different materials for painting. Foil surfaces behave very differently to paper. Great for encouraging discussion and language around the shiny surfaces and the reflected light.

Happy hands (and feet!)

What you need:

No cook version

- **1/3 cup of plain flour**
- **1/3 cup of water**
- **1 tablespoon of glycerin** (available from pharmacy counters)
- **Food colourings** – various colours

What to do:

1. Mix the flour and water well.
2. Add the glycerin and food colouring.
3. Repeat for various colours.
4. Use the paste for finger painting.
5. Dispose of the excess after use.

Taking it forward

- Paint with feet as well as hands.

- Add other textures such as sand, sawdust etc (see Textured Paints page 30).

- Put some finger paint into a sealable food bag and allow the children to squidge patterns and marks in the gel (great for those children who don't like getting their hands in the paint).

What's in it for the children?

Children build up their brain connections for future learning by experiencing the world using all of their senses. This is a great way of giving children the chance to be creative whilst getting fully immersed in a sensory activity.

Top tip ⭐

Add a little washing up liquid to your finger paints to help with washing off afterwards (especially as some food colourings can stain fingers and clothes) but be mindful of skin allergies.

What you need:

Cooked version

- A saucepan
- 2 cups of water
- ½ cup of cornflour
- Food colouring or powder paint
- Paint pots or containers

What to do:

1. Heat the water in saucepan until boiling.

2. Separately, mix the cornflour and a little cold water to make a liquid.

3. Add the cornflour mix to the hot water and simmer for a few minutes, stirring continuously until the mixture forms a clear gel-like paste.

4. Pour into pots dependent upon how many colours you require.

5. Mix in food colouring or powder paint to make required colour.

6. Allow to cool.

7. Use as finger paints.

Health & Safety

For safety reasons this recipe must be prepared by adults prior to children working with it.

Splash it all over!

What you need:

- **Selection of paints of different colours**
- **A small paddling pool**
- **Shaving foam**
- **Selection of different textured tools** (brushes, sticks, combs, pine cones etc)
- **Glitter/sand**
- **Large sheets of paper** (the bigger the better)

Taking it forward

- Why not try letting the children sit in the pool (in old changeable clothes of course!) and explore the paint with their whole bodies – this is great for small children and babies who can sit. Make sure babies are supported and children are supervised as paint makes the surface VERY slippery.

What's in it for the children?

When children experience something for the first time they create new brain connections. When they are given the opportunity to revisit these experiences, they strengthen these connections. Children need to be given lots of opportunities to visit and then revisit their experiences.

Top tip ⭐

Add glitter or sand to the paint for added sensory exploration.

What to do:

The idea of this one is to combine some of the methods used in other sections of the book and allow children to explore on a much bigger scale.

1. Squirt some paints of different colours into the paddling pool.

2. Allow children to kneel beside the pool and move the paint around with their hands.

3. Add shaving foam to the paint to make it thicker (cornflour or flour would work as well).

4. Allow children to make patterns in the paint mixture using fingers, brushes, combs and tools .

5. Place sheets of paper over the paint to pull off a print of their pattern.

Health & Safety

Never put more than a covering of paint in the paddling pool and supervise at all times.

Pebble painting

What you need:

- Acrylic paints in a variety of colours
- Brushes in a variety of small sizes
- A wide variety of pebbles in various colours and sizes
- Baby wipes
- Clear varnish (Yacht varnish is best)

What to do:

This activity gives children an opportunity to explore acrylic paint, which is not often used in early years settings and gives a clear shiny finish.

1. Allow the children to paint their own designs onto pebbles using the acrylic paints.

2. Wiping the brushes with baby wipes in between colour changes will help avoid colours mixing and prolong the life of the brushes.

3. When the pebbles are dry cover them with a coat of varnish to give a shiny, weather resistant covering allowing you to display your pebbles outdoors if you want.

Handy hint

Acrylic paint can stain clothing so supervise carefully and clean off clothes.

Taking it forward

- Allow children to add glitter or googly eyes to their pebble paintings for extra effect.

- Use large boulders for collaborative painting.

- Paint characters onto pebbles and use them as storytelling stones to encourage lots of talk and storytelling fun.

What's in it for the children?

Children need lots of opportunities to explore different types of paints and to paint onto lots of different surfaces. This activity offers an ideal opportunity to paint on unusual materials making the most of outdoor areas, as well as a chance to build on fine motor skills using small brushes for finer details.

Top tip ★

NEVER remove pebbles from the beach yourself — garden centres and DIY stores stock river washed pebbles.

Puddle painting

What you need:

For each colour

- **Powder paint**
- **Some brushes** (loo brushes are ideal – unused of course!), washing up brushes/mops and toothbrushes
- **Puddles** (or make your own if it's not raining!)
- **Large piece of paper**
- **Coloured chalks**
- **Food colouring**
- **Spoons**

Taking it forward

- Use coloured chalks to get more vivid colours in your puddle.
- Use food colouring to get watery effects.
- Try using marbling inks and laying paper onto the surface of the puddle.
- Add some washing up liquid to the puddle and blow using extra long straws (1 meter straws are available from party shops). Lay paper over the top to make a bubbly puddle painting print.

Top tip ★

Have a bucket of soapy water handy to wash away the colour if you don't want a multi-coloured outdoor surface (although it does look great!).

What to do:

1. Take some coloured powder paint and using your brushes and spoons stir it into the puddle.
2. Add another colour and watch as they mix together.
3. Use more water or more paint depending on what consistency the children want the paint.
4. Lay a piece of plain paper over the puddle to take a puddle painting print.
5. Hang your painting on a washing line to dry.

Big it up!

- Use big brushes (DIY ones) and paint rollers with your puddle paint to paint on big sheets of paper on the floor or on old sheets draped on fences.

What's in it for the children?

As outdoor play should be provided all year long in all weathers this offers a great way to enhance play on a rainy day. This is another great way of exploring the varied properties of different materials and observing colour mixing. Mixing up the water with all of those brushes and tools again gives lots of opportunities for building up elbow and shoulder muscles!

Go dotty!

What you need:

- Paint in a variety of colours
- Shallow trays
- Cotton buds
- Paper
- Craft matchsticks

What to do:

1. Pour the paint into the trays.
2. Take a cotton bud and dip it into the paint.
3. Dab repeatedly onto the paper.
4. Go dotty with your creations!

Taking it forward

- Look at and talk about some of the famous painters who use this method (pointillism) including Georges Seurat but don't get the children to copy famous paintings. Looking at famous artists is about exploring processes not producing copies!

- Use fingers instead of cotton buds to make the patterns on the paper.

- Use other small objects to make the dots, including craft matchsticks

- Using mud, clay and chalk paints (see page 20) will create a tribal feel to the paintings which can then be painted onto natural items such as pebbles, shells, sticks and trees. Have a look at some aboriginal paintings for inspiration and discussion (not copying!).

What's in it for the children?

This activity, as well as building their knowledge and understanding of methods used by artists across the world, helps to build those essential fine motor skills needed for writing in later life.

Puffy painting

What you need:

For each colour

- **1 tablespoon of self-raising flour**
- **1 tablespoon of salt**
- **Small amount of water**
- **Food colouring**
- **Brushes and cotton buds**
- **Card pieces** – the thicker the better (cut up card boxes work well and demonstrate recycling at its best!)

What to do:

1. Mix the flour, salt, water and colouring together to make a thick paste.

FOOD allergy !

2. Repeat for other colours until you have a bright selection.

3. Paint onto the card using brushes and cotton buds (you need to keep the paint covering quite thick).

4. Microwave (adults only) the card for 10-30 seconds on full power until the paint puffs up and is dry.

5. Wait for the paintings to cool and admire your puffy paint creations!

Health & Safety
Never let children touch items straight out of the microwave as they are really hot and continue cooking for quite some time.

Taking it forward

- Add some glitter to the paint for sparkly pictures.

- Add silver glitter to plain white mixtures and use black card for a sparkly winter effect.

- Why not try some of the scented effects on page 62? Using the microwave should release the scents.

What's in it for the children?

As well as exploring the multi-sensory nature of this paint mixture (especially if you add scents), this activity gives a great yet unusual chance to see how some materials change when you heat them.

Top tip ⭐

Microwave in 10 second blasts as all machines are different and this prevents your pictures burning.

Salty paint

What you need:

For each colour

- **Paper** – white and black
- **Glue sticks**
- **Salt** (if you can get different types and textures such as sea salt and table salt then even better!)
- **Paint brushes**
- **Water-based colour paints** (or powder paints mixed to a watery consistency)
- **Food colourings**

What to do:

Method 1

1. On the black paper make a picture with your glue stick – the swirlier the better!
2. Sprinkle table salt onto the glue to cover it.
3. Shake off and then re-use any excess salt.
4. Use a paintbrush to drop some water-based colour paint or food colouring onto the salty pattern.
5. Watch as the colour bleeds through the salt
6. Add more paint in different colours – watch the colours mix as they meet.
7. Allow to dry.

Top tip ⭐

Rock salt with larger granules works better for this activity.

What to do:

Method 2

1. Using the water colour washes, paint onto white paper (making sure that the pictures are quite wet).

2. Sprinkle on some salt.

3. Watch as the salt absorbs the coloured water in the paint and makes crystal type patterns.

4. Allow to dry.

Taking it forward

- Mix a tiny bit of food colouring with salt (not enough so that it completely dissolves but enough to colour the salt). Let the salt dry out again and use coloured salt in the two methods above.

Big it up!

Use coloured salt (see opposite page) to make patterns on frosty or snowy surfaces outside – what happens to the snow and frost?

What's in it for the children?

A great way of exploring the properties of different materials and observing what happens when they are mixed together. A lovely chance to explore colour mixing. Early science creativity at its best!

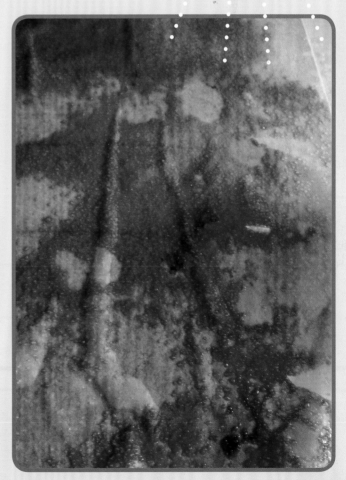

> ### Top tip ⭐
>
> Using washes with food colouring and a little water can make colours more vivid.

Spiky prickly patterns

What you need:

- **Paint in a variety of colours** (thicker poster paint works better than watery powder paint)
- **Tea trays**
- **Sponges or large sponges dabbers and brushes**
- **A selection of spiky, prickly objects** including brushes, combs, pencils, sticks, straws, fir cones, dabbers, dish mops, toothbrushes, dish scourers, bath body scrubbers etc.
- **Paper**

What to do:

1. Pour paint onto the tray and move it around with a sponge or brush until there is a thick layer covering the surface of the tray.
2. Use various spiky items to scrape through the paint leaving patterns.
3. Place paper carefully over the surface of the tray and smooth down gently.
4. Remove the paper to reveal a relief print of your picture.

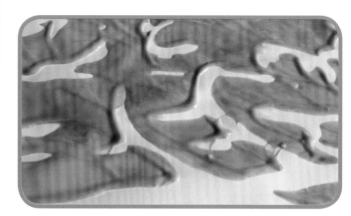

Taking it forward

- Try a similar activity with mud and clay paint and natural objects such as sticks, twigs, pine cones, grass etc to make the patterns (a relief print can still be taken on paper).
- Use fingers to make the patterns in the paint and take prints.
- Can the children draw their initials in the paint and take a print?

Top tip ⭐

The paint needs to be really thick. Consider adding flour or cellulose paste (non fungicidal) to make it even thicker.

Big it up!

Try this on a bigger scale in a builder's tray or a paddling pool. With large pieces of paper you can get great oversized prints and this provides an ideal opportunity to work together to produce a shared pattern.

What's in it for the children?

This activity, along with giving children great opportunities to mark make and explore pattern making, helps them to investigate the nature of paint and its many squishy properties, as well as developing an understanding of simple printing skills.

 54

Splish, splash, flick!

What you need:

- **Paint in a variety of colours** (thicker poster paint works better than watery powder paint)
- **Shallow trays** (takeaway containers are ideal)
- **A selection of bristly items** including nail brushes, toothbrushes, scrubbing brushes, toilet brushes (all new of course!)
- **Paper**
- **Masking tape**

What to do:

1. Pour the paint into the trays/containers.
2. Dip one of the bristly items into the paint so the bristles are covered.
3. Turning the bristles upwards, hold them so they are tilted towards the paper.
4. Run your fingers along the bristles (away from you) allowing the paint to flick onto the paper.
5. Change the colour or use a different brush and try again.
7. You end up with a splatter picture which can be as colourful as you want it.

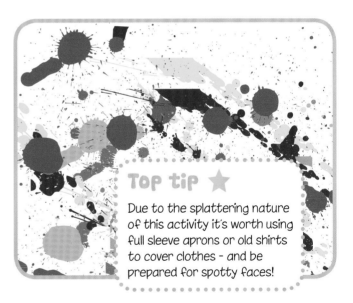

Top tip ★

Due to the splattering nature of this activity it's worth using full sleeve aprons or old shirts to cover clothes - and be prepared for spotty faces!

Taking it forward

- Try using black paper and fluorescent or shiny paints.
- Flick the paint on the objects as well as the bristles. Run your finger along the bristles so that the paint flicks and see if you can make some extra patterns.
- Try flicking paint onto cheap canvases (very Jackson Pollock! and an ideal opportunity to introduce the children to some of his paintings).

Big it up!

Stick a few large pieces of paper together with masking tape to make a huge piece of paper. Now use all the brushes outside to really flick paint at the paper using an over arm action. A great way to build upper arm muscles ready for later writing skills!

What's in it for the children?

The different levels of this activity use different arm muscles from small wrist movements as they brush the bristles, to larger elbow and shoulder movements, as they get big flicking motion going. All of this builds hand-eye and motor skills essential to pre-writing development.

Swirly swing painting

What you need:

- A selection of clean yoghurt pots or plastic/polystyrene cups
- String
- Masking tape
- Watered down paint in various colours
- A broom handle or long stick
- Paper

Taking it forward

- Try using pots with different length strings and different sized holes.

Big it up!

- Attach two or three pots to a broom handle or a long stick and hold over a big sheet of paper on the floor. Alternatively, tie the strings onto a washing line strung above the paper. Fill the pots with paint and swing away.

- Try using a bucket with a big hole in it over a REALLY big piece of paper!

What's in it for the children?

This is a great way to explore the properties of paint as well as watching the motion of the pots as they move. Children love seeing the smaller and smaller swings as the pots slow down.

What to do:

1. Make a hole in the bottom of a couple of pots/cups using a pencil (adult activity).

2. Loop string around the neck or top of the pot/cup so that the pot dangles freely on the end of the string. To get the pot to hang straight you may need two pieces of string on either side of the pot.

3. Place a piece of masking tape over the hole in the pot (on the outside).

4. Put some watered down paint into the pot.

5. With one hand hold the string ends and lift the pot into the air.

6. Ask someone to take the tape off the bottom allowing the paint to flow through the hole onto the paper below. Now slowly swing the pot to make patterns. Can you make the pot swing in a circle?

7. Try again with other colours.

Top tip ⭐

Watered down paint is less likely to block the hole in the pot and allow paint to flow better.

Tyre and wheel painting

What you need:

- Large sheets of paper and/or a large white sheet
- Masking tape
- Selection of different coloured poster paints
- Large trays or builder's trays
- Selection of old tyres and wheels from cars, bikes and old outdoor toys

Taking it forward

- Try and find other things to roll across the paper. Footballs, tennis balls, beach balls and spiky balls are all great as are pine cones and acorns.

Going small

- Why not go the opposite scale and try roller painting with marbles and acorns etc on tea trays (see page 58).

What's in it for the children?

A great way to get creative on a massive scale and as well as helping to develop gross motor skills and build on co-operative working.

Top tip ⭐

This activity produces an end product which is on a grand scale. Wherever possible, try to display it somewhere even for a short time - it will look great surrounded by photos of the children painting it!

What to do:

1. Stick plenty of sheets of paper together using masking tape to make a massive single canvas and lay it out on a flat surface outdoors. Alternatively, spread out a large white sheet and anchor the edges using logs or pebbles.

2. Place large amounts of paint into a flat tray. Builder's trays are ideal as are large seed trays or plastic boot trays (the kind for protecting the carpet in your hallway).

3. Roll a tyre or wheel in the paint being sure to cover the tread all over. Roll the tyre over to ensure good coverage.

4. Now roll the tyre or wheel across the paper and see the patterns of the tread appear on the paper.

5. Can your friend catch the wheel at the other side of the paper and roll it back?

6. What happens when you use different coloured paints and they begin to mix as you roll?

7. Look for different patterns on different tyres.

Health & Safety

Make sure to supervise at all times and that the tyres are not too big for children to handle.

On a roll

What you need:

- Water-based paint in a variety of colours
- Paper
- A selection of objects which roll including balls, marbles, cotton reels, ping pong balls, spiky balls and corks
- Trays with lips (round or rectangular tea trays are ideal)

What to do:

Draw around the tray bottom onto the paper and cut out so you have a piece of paper which fits snuggly into the tray.

Approach 1

1. Pour some paint onto the paper (about the size of a 50p will do). Do this a few times with different colours in different parts of the tray.

2. Put an object onto the tray.

3. Hold the tray and carefully tip it so that the object rolls through the paint and leaves a colourful trail behind it. Can you tip the tray so that all of the colours start to mix?

Taking it forward

- Use black paper and fluorescent or shiny paints.

- Try with natural objects such as conkers, fir cones, pebbles and mud and clay paints as an outdoor activity.

Using trays with hand holes makes it easier for the children to grip.

Big it up!

Why not get a big white sheet, dip a selection of large balls (tennis, footballs, basketballs etc) into the paint. Stand around the outside of the sheet and together pull the sheet tight (a bit like using a parachute for play). Now add the balls to the middle of the sheet and work together to move the paint covered ball backwards and forward making a lovely large scale painting. Great for creative teamwork and building communication skills!

What's in it for the children?

As well as developing hand-eye coordination skills as they tip the tray to make the objects move, this activity is a great way of children exploring objects that roll and how tipping at different angles can make them roll slower or faster.

Top tip ★

Put some sticky tack under the paper to stop it moving as you tip the tray.

What to do:

Approach 2

1. Paint directly onto the objects and then place them onto the paper (try more than one object at a time).

2. Tip the tray and watch the patterns emerge on the paper.

3. Add more objects with more colours and watch the colours mix as you roll.

Squirty painting

What you need:

For each colour:

- **Paint in a variety of colours**
- **Water**
- **Empty washing up liquid bottles**
- **Empty water spray bottles with triggers** (available cheaply from most pound shops)
- **Pegs or pins** (to attach the sheet to a fence or wall to create a vertical surface)
- **An old sheet** – preferably white

What to do:

1. Mix up the paint and water to a watery but brightly coloured solution.
2. Pour into the bottles.
3. Peg the sheet to a fence or wall.
4. Spray/squirt away to your heart's content!

Taking it forward

- Try using the same method on large oversized pieces of paper on the floor.

What's in it for the children?

Another great way to get creative outdoors in all weathers. This activity offers children the chance to explore new methods and tools for painting, as well as painting on a much bigger scale than they are used to. A great one for encouraging social skills and group interactions.

Top tip ⭐

Don't make the paint too thick or it will block the nozzle of the spray. Use water-soluble paint and the sheet can be washed and reused on another day.

Stick and tree painting

What you need:

- **Chalk or clay paints made from mixing small amounts with water** (chalk makes lovely white paint, clay a wide variety of colours).

- **A variety of brushes and dabbers** including grass brushes (see page 16). **Lots of sticks of various sizes and thicknesses** (different trees have different coloured barks)

- **Log slices** (available from a local tree surgeon)

- **Logs of various different shapes and sizes**

- **Mud paint** (see page 20)

Taking it forward

- Use a really big log slice to make a group painting.

- Stand sticks in the ground and top off with painted terracotta flowerpots to decorate your outdoor area (if you fill the flowerpots with straw they make a great winter hide out for minibeasts).

- Try painting onto other natural materials such as bark (see page 21), pine cones or pebbles (see page 47)

Top tip ★

Try grinding red house brick with a pestle and mortar and mixing the powder with water - it makes a great bright orange/red paint.

What to do:

1. Encourage children to paint onto the cut end of the logs and log slices using brushes, dabbers or just their fingers. The use of natural mud and clay paints gives a primitive tribal feel to the paintings.

2. Sticks can be dipped into paint as well as having patterns painted on to them.

3. When dry, use the painted logs to decorate your outdoor area or as colourful seating for a quite corner.

Health & Safety

Check the logs for splinters before you start.

Big it up!

- Combine stick paintings and string with bark painting (see page 21) to make your own painted wind mobile. Add feathers and leaves for added effect.

What's in it for the children?

This activity gives children an opportunity to explore painting with new and exciting materials as part of fun, hands-on outdoor activities. It's important to give children the opportunity to be creative both indoors and outdoors.

Did you know?

Some children will talk more outdoors than they will indoors.

Smelly paint

What you need:

- Poster or powder paint in a variety of colours
- Range of smelly materials including: toothpaste, lavender, orange essence, lemon essence or lemon zest, vanilla essence (a chocolaty smell), perfume, coffee essence or coffee grounds, strawberry essence, lime zest, almond essence (smells like marzipan), chopped herbs such as basil, mint or curry plant.
- Brushes, sponges and dabbers
- Paper of various colours shapes and sizes

What to do:

1. Mix up the scented materials with different coloured paints until the smell is easily distinguishable.
2. Allow children to paint as they would with unscented paints.
3. Encourage children to talk about what they can smell as they are painting.

SKIN allergy!

FOOD allergy!

Health & Safety
It's important to emphasise that paint is not edible no matter how good it smells!

Taking it forward

- Let the children have a go at mixing their own smelly paints and combining scents as well as blending and mixing colours.
- Let the paintings dry and see if they can still identify any of the smells in the paintings?

Big it up!

Why not use chopped up aromatic herbs that you have grown in your own outdoor garden to make lots of smelly paint mixtures outside. Use big oversized spoons to create really big smell paint mixtures. Try adding some glitter for extra paint magic!

What's in it for the children?

This activity involves lots of multi-sensory stimulation that helps to build new brain connections and also allows children to explore the use of their senses in a wide variety of situations. Also lots of opportunity for language development whilst mixing and exploring the changing properties of the paints.

Did you know?

Approximately 80% of what we taste is actually attributed to our sense of smell.

Our sense of taste is limited to just five sensations: salty, sweet, bitter, sour and savoury. All of the other flavours that we taste are actually determined by our sense of smell. That's the reason why food tastes bland when we have a blocked nose due to a cold or flu.

Water painting

What you need:

- Brushes, sponges, rollers, dabbers and dish mops
- Buckets and roller trays full of water
- A wall or playground surface

What to do:

1. Dip the brushes etc into the water.
2. Paint directly onto a variety of surfaces – make available concrete, wood and chalk board surfaces.
3. Offer this opportunity on sunny, rainy and frosty days with different effects. (On sunny days watch the picture disappear as water evaporates – does it do the same when it's not sunny?)

Health & Safety

Always take care with water on surfaces when it's freezing outdoors.

Taking it forward

- Colour the water with food colouring or a small amount of paint.
- Try painting onto frosty surfaces with warm water.
- Use coloured water paints to brush or spray onto snow for a colourful outdoor winter activity.
- Let the water paint dry and see if you can still identify any of the shapes you made.
- Try filling squirty bottles and squirting at the floor or a large piece of paper.

Big it up!

Why not allow children to paint with water and full-sized mops directly onto playgrounds and other hard surfaces?

What's in it for the children?

As well as exploring some of the many properties of water, children get the opportunity to mark make on a larger scale than usual. Lots of early science exploration occurs as children watch the process of evaporation or melting (of frost and snow).

Did you know?

Mark making using bigger, exaggerated body movements helps build muscles and muscle control in shoulders, elbows and wrists – all of which are essential to motor skills used in early writing.